I0437038

The Story of a Special Day
Volume 66

March 6

65th day of the year
(66th in leap years)
300 days remaining
until the end of the year.

by Michael Dobson

Timespinner
Press

For more information about the series, about me, or
about your special day, please email us at
editor@timespinnerpress.com.

Look for other volumes in *The Story of a Special Day,*
coming often.

Table of Contents

Cover: The Alamo lit by the sun, in honor of the final day of Battle of the Alamo, March 6, 1836.

March 6 Quotations

"If you knew how much work went into it, you would not call it genius."
— *Michelangelo, born March 6, 1475*

"You imagine that what you cannot understand is either spiritual or does not exist. The conclusion is quite wrong; rather there are obviously a million things in the universe that we would need a million quite different organs to understand."
— *Cyrano de Bergerac, born March 6, 1619*

"How do I love thee? Let me count the ways. I love thee to the depth and breadth and height my soul can reach..."
— *Elizabeth Barrett Browning, born March 6, 1806*

"I guess I should warn you, if I turn out to be particularly clear, you've probably misunderstood what I said."
— *Alan Greenspan, chairman of the Federal Reserve, born March 6, 1926*

"Ultimately, literature is nothing but carpentry."
— Gabriel García Márquez, born March 6, 1927

"All work is an act of philosophy."
— Ayn Rand, died March 6, 1982

"An intelligent, energetic, educated woman cannot be kept in four walls — even satin-lined, diamond-studded walls — without discovering sooner or later that they are still a prison cell.
— Pearl S. Buck, died March 6, 1973

"First they came for the socialists, and I didn't speak out because I wasn't a socialist. Then they came for the trade unionists, and I didn't speak out because I wasn't a trade unionist. Then they came for the Jews, and I didn't speak out because I wasn't a Jew. Then they came for me, and there was no one left to speak for me.
— Martin Niemöller, died March 6, 1984

The Battle of the Alamo

In the early morning hours of March 6, 1836, a Mexican force of 1,500 soldiers under the command of President General Antonio López de Santa Anna advanced on a small garrison of Texians holed up in a former Roman Catholic mission known as the Alamo, which had been converted to a makeshift fort.

Several months earlier, Texian forces had driven Mexican troops out of what was then Mexican Texas. Santa Anna marched his army north to bring the territory back under Mexican control. On February 23, 1836, his forces reached San Antonio and laid siege to the small garrison.

Knowing the strategic importance of San Antonio, the Alamo's defenders had been pleading for men and supplies. Unfortunately, the provisional Texian government wasn't in a position to provide much help. Reinforcements trickled in slowly. Colonel James Bowie arrived with 30 men, and calvary officer William B.

Travis brought 30 more. Another small group of volunteers showed up a few days after Travis, led by frontiersman and former U. S. Congressman Davy Crockett of Tennessee.

The siege began with cannon fire, and slowly the Mexican forces began to take up positions closer to the fort, as well as block the roads that might carry reinforcements. Over 600 additional Mexican troops joined the 1,500 already present.

On March 6, the battle began in earnest. Two Mexican Army attacks were repulsed, but the third attack reached the walls of the Alamo itself. As Mexican soldiers scaled the walls, the Texian defenders withdrew into interior buildings while their artillery continued to fire. Lacking ammunition, the Alamo defenders began loading their cannons with door hinges, nails, and chopped-up horseshoes.

It was to no avail. While the battle raged on into the night, the overwhelming Mexican force could not be stopped. By 6:30am the following morning, the battle was over. A handful of noncombatant Texians were spared; the remainder of the approximately 200 Alamo defenders perished. Between 400 and 600 Mexican soldiers died in the battle.

While at the time, Santa Anna considered the Battle of the Alamo to be a minor episode in his attempt to reconquer Mexican Texas, the fate of the Alamo defenders had the opposite effect on the Texian cause. Soldiers flocked to the army of Sam Houston, and at the Battle of San Jacinto on April 21, the Texian army took Santa Anna's forces by surprise, defeating them in about 18 minutes.

It was during that battle that the cry, "Remember the Alamo!" first rang out, giving rise to both historical and mythological portrayals that have shaped American and Texan culture ever since.

"The Fall of the Alamo," by Robert Jenkins Onderdonk

March 6 Holidays and Celebrations

Foundation Day (Territory of Norfolk Island)

On March 6, 1788, British Navy Lieutenant Philip Gidley King landed on Norfolk Island, an uninhabited small island located between Australia, New Zealand, and New Caledonia, and established the First Fleet settlement there, consisting of 22 people including 15 convicts. This occasion is celebrated as Foundation Day, and includes a reenactment of the landing.

Flag of the Territory of Norfolk Island

Independence Day (Ghana)

The West African nation of Ghana, known as the Gold Coast when it was a British colony, achieved its independence from Great Britain on March 6, 1957, the first independent black African nation to emerge from the colonial era.

Flag of the Republic of Ghana

Christian Feast Days

Saints commemorated on March 5 include Chrodegang, Colette, Fridolin, Kyneburga, Kyneswide, Tibba, Marcian of Tortona, and Olegarius.

What Happened on March 6?

1820 CE – Missouri Compromise Becomes Law

With anti-slavery and pro-slavery factions at loggerheads, the United States Congress struggled with the fate of slavery in the new Louisiana Territory. The compromise established Missouri as a slave state (balanced by the admission of Maine as a free state), but prohibited slavery in the northern portions of the new American lands. This temporary compromise did little to hold back the increasing conflict between slave and free states that eventually led to the American Civil War.

1857 CE – Dred Scott Decision

In the case of Dred Scott v. Sandford, slave Dred Scott sued for his freedom because he had been taken to the Wisconsin territory, where slavery was forbidden under the Missouri Compromise. When the case reached the Supreme Court, it ruled against Scott on March 6, 1857, declaring not only that people of African descent were not citizens of the U.S., regardless of whether they were slaves, but also ruled the Missouri Compromise itself unconstitutional. The controvery from this decision helped start the political career of Abraham Lincoln and is considered a critical moment in the events leading to the Civil War.

Portrait of Dred Scott by Louis Schultze, 1888

1867 CE – First Periodic Table

Russian chemist and inventor Дмитрий Менделе́ев (Dmitri Mendeleev) created the first version of the periodic table of elements, consisting of the 56 known elements. The periodic table enabled him to predict the properties of elements still to be discovered. He revealed his new table in a presentation before the Russian Chemical Society on March 6, 1867. Element 101, mendelevium, is named for him.

1912 CE – Oreo Cookies Introduced

According to manufacturer Kraft Foods/Nabisco, the Oreo sandwich cookie was first introduced on March 6, 1912. Although it was an imitation of the Hydrox cookie, Oreo soon surpassed the original and is now the best-seling cookie in the United States.

1951 CE – Rosenberg Trial Begins

On March 6, 1951, the trial of Julius and Ethel Rosenberg, American communists accused of passing atomic bomb secrets to the Soviet Union, began. They were convicted and executed on June 19, 1953, the only American civilians executed for espionage in U. S. history.

1962 CE – Ash Wednesday Storm

The "Ash Wednesday" storm of 1962 hit the mid-Atlantic coast on March 6, 1962. One of the ten worst storms in the U.S. in the 20th century, it killed 40, injured over 1,000, and caused hundreds of million dollars in damage, primarily in North Carolina and Virginia.

1964 CE – Cassius Clay Becomes Muhammad Ali

On March 6, 1964, Nation of Islam leader Elijah Muhammad officially gave boxing champion Cassius Clay the new name of Muhammad Ali, signifying his conversion to Islam.

Muhammad Ali

1967 CE – Stalin's Daughter Defects

On March 6, 1967, the daughter of Soviet dictator Joseph Stalin, Svetlana Alliluyeva (Светлáна Аллилýева), walked into the United

12

States Embassy in New Delhi, India, and requested political asylum in the United States.

1981 CE – Cronkite Signs Off

CBS anchorman Walter Cronkite, named "the most trusted man in America" in an opinion poll, signed off for the last time with his trademark phrase, "And that's the way it is: Friday, March 6, 1981."

Walter Cronkite, 1976

Who Was Born on March 6?

The abbreviation "O.S." on some dates refers to the fact that the Russian Empire did not switch from the Julian to the Gregorian calendar at the same time as the rest of Europe, and therefore some figures have two dates for their birth or death.

People whose original names are not in the Western alphabet have their native names in the appropriate script shown in parenthesis.

Acting

Moira Kelly (March 6, 1968 —)

Actress Moira Kelly was in the 1992 film *The Cutting Edge,* had feature roles in the television shows *One Tree Hill* and *West Wing,* and voiced Nala in Disney's *The Lion King.*

Connie Britton (March 6, 1967 —)

Connie Britton received two Emmy nominations for her role in television's *Friday Night Lights.* She also had featured roles in the TV series *Spin City* and *Nashville.*

Yvette Wilson (March 6, 1964 — June 14, 2012)

Yvette Wilson began her career in the UPN sitcom *Moesha* and went on to appear in numerous comedy films as well as on *Def Comedy Jam*.

D. L. Hughley (March 6, 1963 —)

Actor and stand-up comedian D. L. Hughley starred in the eponymous sitcom *The Hughleys* and was featured in Spike Lee's film *The Original Kings of Comedy*.

Suzanne Crough (March 6, 1963 —)

Suzanne Crough is best known as Tracy Partridge from the TV sitcom *The Partridge Family*.

Tom Arnold (March 6, 1959 —)

Actor and comedian Tom Arnold is best known as Rosanne Barr's husband, and has appeared in a number of films, most notably 1994's *True Lies*.

Eddie Deezen (March 6, 1957 —)

Famous for playing stereotypical nerd characters in such films as *Grease* and *WarGames*, Deezen is also a voice artist known for the character

Mandark in the animated series *Dexter's Laboratory* and as Lenny the Know-It-All in the film *The Polar Express.*

Rob Reiner (March 6, 1947 —)

Originally known as "Meathead" in the 1970s television series *All in the Family,* Rob Reiner went on to prominence as a director and producer, nominated for Directors Guild Awards for his films *Stand by Me, When Harry Met Sally...,* and *A Few Good Men.*

Anna Maria Horsford (March 6, 1948 —)

Actress Anna Maria Horsford had feature roles on the television series *Amen, The Wayans Bros.,* and *Reed Between the Lines,* and appeared in the comedy film *Friday* and its sequel.

Martin Kove (March 6, 1960 —)

Actor Martin Kove is best known for his role as the dojo instructor in *The Karate Kid* who ordered one of his students to "sweep the leg."

Ben Murphy (March 6, 1942 —)

Ben Murphy co-starred in the ABC television series *Alias Smith and Jones.*

Hal Needham (March 6, 1931 —)

Top stuntman Hal Needham also wrote and directed such films as *Smokey and the Bandit, Hooper,* and *Cannonball Run.*

Ed McMahon (March 6, 1923 — June 23, 2009)

Most famous as Johnny Carson's sidekick on *The Tonight Show* from 1962 to 1992, Ed McMahon was also known as the face of sweepstakes marketers American Family Publishers.

Lewis Gilbert (March 6, 1920 —)

British director and producer Lewis Gilbert directed three classic James Bond films, *You Only Live Twice, The Spy Who Loved Me,* and *Moonraker.*

Lou Costello (March 6, 1906 — March 3, 1959)

Chubby comedian Lou Costello was best known as half of the comedy duo Abbott and Costello, and for his trademark phrase, "Heyyyy, Abbott!"

Lou Costello (left) with Hillary Brooke in *Africa Screams*

Business and Crime

Ivan Boesky (March 6, 1937 —)

American stock trader Ivan Boesky served two years in prison as part of his role in a Wall Street insider trading scandal of the mid-1980s.

Music and Dance

Julio Bocca (March 6, 1967 —)

Named one of the most important ballet dancers of the late 20th century and perhaps the most important Argentine dancer of all time, Julio Bocca has danced with the American Ballet Theater, the Royal Ballet, and the Bolshoi Ballet. He has won numerous prestigious competitions including the International Ballet Competition and the International Gold Medal.

Skip Ewing (March 6, 1964 —)

Country music singer Skip Ewing has appeared on the *Billboard* country charts fifteen times.

Stephen Schwartz (March 6, 1948 —)

Lyricist and composer Stephen Schwartz wrote hit musicals including *Godspell, Pippin,* and *Wicked,* along with lyrics for Disney films including *Pocahontas, The Hunchback of Notre Dame,* and *Enchanted.* He has won six Grammys, three Academy Aards, and the Drama Desk Award for Outstanding Lyrics.

Kiki Dee (March 6, 1947 —)

British singer Kiki Dee is best known for her 1976 hit duet with Elton John, "Don't Go Breaking My Heart."

David Gilmour (March 6, 1946 —)

Pink Floyd guitarist, singer, and songwriter David Gilmour was named CBE (Commander of the Order of the British Empire) for his charity work. *Rolling Stone* ranks him as the 14th greatest guitarist of all time.

The Supremes, 1966 (from left to right: Florence Ballard, Mary Wilson, Diana Ross)

Mary Wilson (March 6, 1944 —)

A founding member of the Motown group The Supremes, she was the only consistent member of the group during its eighteen-year existence.

Kiri Te Kanawa (March 6, 1944 —)

International opera star Kiri Te Kanawa was created a Dame Commander of the Order of the British Empire (DBE) in 1982.

Flora Purim (March 6, 1942 —)

Brazilian jazz singer Flora Purim is best known for her work on Chick Corea's 1972 album *Return to Forever.* She received Brazil's Ordem do Rio Branco for Lifetime Achievement in 2002.

Wes Montgomery (March 6, 1923 — June 15, 1968)

Legendary jazz guitarist Wes Montgomery began his career touring with Lionel Hampton's orchestra. As a solo artist, he is considered a great influence on subsequent generations of guitarists and won two Grammy awards.

Bob Wills (March 6, 1905 — May 13, 1975)

Known as the King of Western Swing, Bob Wills and his band the Texas Playboys had numerous hits in the 1940s, and were inducted into the Rock and Roll Hall of Fame in 1999.

Military

Georg Luger (March 6, 1849 — December 22, 1923)

Austrian designer Georg Luger designed the eponymous pistol and the 9x19mm parabellum cartridge.

Philip Sheridan (March 6, 1831 — August 5, 1888)

Union Civil War General Philip Sheridan led the cavalry corps of the Army of the Potomac, defeating Confederate forces in the Shenandoah Valley. He was instrumental in forcing the surrender of Robert E. Lee at Appomatox.

Politics and Newsmakers

John Stossel (March 6, 1947 —)

Journalist and author John Stossel hosts a weekly news show on Fox Business, *Stossel,* and appears on numerous other Fox News programs. He has won 19 Emmy Awards for his work.

Christopher "Kit" Bond (March 6, 1939 —)

Kit Bond served two terms as Governor of Missouri and three terms as U. S. Senator from Missouri.

Marion Barry, Jr. (March 6, 1936 —)

Second elected mayor of Washington, DC, prominent civil rights activist Marion Barry, Jr., notoriously was caught on video smoking crack cocaine and served six months in Federal prison. After his release, he was re-elected to the DC City Council

Marion Barry

23

and subsequently served a third term as mayor beginning in 1995.

Alan Greenspan (March 6, 1926 —)

Former chairman of the Federal Reserve, Alan Greenspan was the second-longest serving person in that role.

William H. Webster (March 6, 1924 —)

Former Federal judge William H. Webster served as director of the FBI from 1978 to 1987 and as Director of Central Intelligence from 1987 to 1991.

Empress Kōjun (香淳皇后) (March 6, 1903 — June 16, 2000)

Empress consort of the Shōwa Emperor (better known in the West as Emperor Hirohito), Empress Kōjun, known as Nagako during her lifetime, was the longest-lived empress consort in Japanese history.

Henry Laurens (March 6, 1724 [O.S. February 24, 1723] — December 8, 1792)

South Carolina slave-trader and rice planter Henry Laurens succeeded John Hancock as President of the Congress during the

Revolutionary War and served as Vice-President of South Carolina under the Articles of Confederation.

Henry Laurens

John of Gaunt, 1st Duke of Lancaster (March 6, 1340 — February 3, 1399)

Younger brother of Edward, the Black Prince, John of Gaunt was a highly influential member of the House of Plantagenet and with a fortune equivalent to $110 billion today, the sixteenth richest man in history. His heirs, the House of Lancaster, included Kings Henry IV, Henry V, and Henry VI.

Science and Space

Carolyn Porco (March 6, 1953 —)

Named one of *Time* magazine's 50 most influential people in space, planetary scientist Carolyn Porco is known for her work in the exploration of the outer solar system. She was awarded the Carl Sagan Medal in 2010.

Valentina Tereshkova (Валентина Терешко́ва) (March 6, 1937 —)

Cosmonaut Valentina Tereshkova is the first woman to have flown in space. She piloted the Vostok 6 mission in 1963.

Valentina Tereshkova

Gordon Cooper (March 6, 1927 — October 4, 2004)

One of the seven original Project Mercury astronauts, Gordon Cooper piloted the longest and final Mercury spaceflight in 1963 and served as command pilot of the Gemini 5 mission.

Gordon Cooper

Joseph von Fraunhofer (March 6, 1787 — June 7, 1826)

German optician Joseph von Fraunhofer discovered the dark absorption lines in the solar spectrum, named Fraunhofer lines in his honor.

Sports

Shaquille O'Neal (March 6, 1972 —)

Basketball superstar Shaquille O'Neal, nicknamed "Shaq," ranks 6th all-time in points scored, 5th in field goals, 13th in rebounds, and 7th in blocks in his 19-year professional career.

Shaquille O'Neal

Erika Hess (March 6, 1962 —)

Swiss alpine skiier Erika Hess won 31 World Cup victories, six World Championship gold medals, and a bronze in the 1980 Winter Olympics.

Sleepy Floyd (March 6, 1960 —)

NBA All-Star Sleepy Floyd holds the NBA playoff record for points scored in a quarter (29) and in a half (39).

Dick Fosbury (March 6, 1947 —)

Track and field athlete Dick Fosbury revolutionized the high jump event with his technique known as the "Fosbury Flop," winning the gold and setting a record at the 1968 Olympics. He serves as president of the World Olympians Association.

Willie Stargell (March 6, 1940 — April 9, 2001)

Baseball hall of famer Willie Stargell played his entire 21-year career as the left fielder and first baseman for the Pittsburgh Pirates.

Lefty Grove (March 6, 1900 — May 22, 1975)

Left-handed pitcher Lefty Grove won the pitcher's Triple Crown twice, and was elected to the Baseball Hall of Fame in 1974.

Words and Pictures

Jeff Greenwald (March 6, 1954 —)

Best-selling author and monologist Jeff Greenwald is known for his travel writing, such as 1990's *Shopping for Buddhas,* and as co-founder of the organization Ethical Travel.

Richard Corliss (March 6, 1944 —)

Best known as the film critic for *Time* magazine, Richard Corliss is also the former editor-in-chief of *Film Comment.*

Gabriel García Márquez (March 6, 1927 —)

Nobel Prize winning author Gabriel García Márquez is considered one of the most important authors of the 20th century, known for such works as *One Hundred Years of Solitude* and *Love in the Time of Cholera.*

Will Eisner (March 6, 1917 — January 3, 2005)

Comic book pioneer Will Eisner is famous for his long-running and highly influential comic *The Spirit* and as the leading force in establishing the graphic novel as a form of literature with his book *A Contract With God and Other Tenement Stories*. The Will Eisner Comic Industry Awards and the Will Eisner Comic Book Hall of Fame are named for him.

Will Eisner's *The Spirit*

Ring Lardner (March 6, 1885 — September 25, 1933)

Sports columnist and short story writer Ring Lardner was best known for his satirical takes on the sports world.

Elizabeth Barrett Browning (March 6, 1806 — June 29, 1861)

Elizabeth Barrett Browning was one of the most prominent Victorian era poets, best known for her sonnet "How do I Love Thee?" Her husband was poet Robert Browning

Elizabeth Barrett Browning

Cyrano de Bergerac (March 6, 1619 — July 28, 1655)

Playwright and soldier Cyrano de Bergerac wrote some of the earliest known works of science fiction. Today, he is best known for the play written loosely about his life by Edmund Rostand. Although de Bergerac's nose was rather large, it was by no means the honker described in the play.

Michelangelo (March 6, 1475 — February 18, 1564)

Michelangelo di Lodovico Buonarroti Simoni, best known by his first name, is one of the essential figures in the history of Western art. One of the dominant figures of the Italian Renaissance, Michelangelo was a sculptor, a painter, an architect, a poet, and an engineer. His masterpieces include the statues *Pietá* and *David,* the frescoes in the Sistine Chapel, and the dome of St. Peter's Basilica in Rome.

"The Creation of Man," Sistine Chapel Ceiling, by Michelangelo

Who Died on March 6?

Acting

Dana Reeve (March 17, 1961 — March 6, 2006)

Widow of Superman actor Christopher Reeve, actress and singer Dana Reeve died less than two years after her husband, who had become a quadriplegic as a result of a riding accident.

Teresa Wright (October 27, 1918 — March 6, 2005)

Winner of the Academy Award for Best Supporting Actress in 1942 for her role in *Mrs. Miniver,* actress Teresa Wright also appeared in such films as *Pride of the Yankees, Shadow of a Doubt,* and *The Best Years of Our Lives.*

Teresa Wright

Melina Mercouri (Μελίνα Μερκούρη) (July 28, 1924 — March 6, 2006)

Melina Mercouri starred in such films as *Never on Sunday* and *Topkapi,* winning the award for Best Actress at the 1960 Cannes Film Festival. She later became the first female Minister of Culture in Greece.

William Hopper (January 26, 1915 — March 6, 1970)

Son of gossip columnist Hedda Hopper, William Hopper is best known for his role as private investigator Paul Drake in the long-running television series *Perry Mason.*

Margaret Dumont (October 20, 1882 — March 6, 1965)

Margaret Dumont is remembered as the comic foil to Groucho Marx in such films as *Duck Soup, A Night at the Opera,* and *A Day at the Races.*

Art

Georgia O'Keeffe (November 15, 1887 — March 6, 1986)

One of the most important American artists of the 20th century, Georgia O'Keeffe's work is displayed in museums throughout the country.

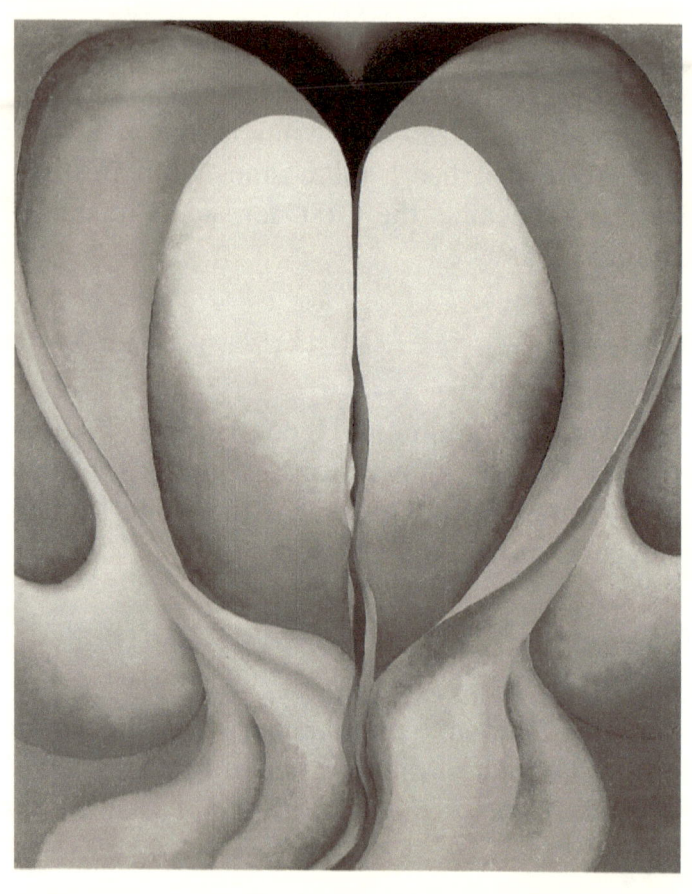

Series 1, No. 8 by Georgia O'Keeffe

Gutzon Borglum (March 25, 1867 — March 6, 1941)

Gutzon Borglum is best known for creating the monuments at Mount Rushmore and Stone Mountain.

Construction of George Washington's head at Mount Rushmore

Business

Ernest Gallo (March 18, 1909 — March 6, 2007)

Ernest Gallo co-founded the E & J Gallo Winery, the largest exporter of California wines, with his brother Julio. Beginning with $5,900 in borrowed money in 1933, the brothers became billionaires through their wine-making and distributing company.

Gottlieb Daimler (March 17, 1834 — March 6, 1900)

Engineer and industrialist Gottlieb Daimler invented the high-speed petrol engine and the first four-wheel automobile. With his partner Wilhelm Maybach, he founded the Daimler Motors Corporation, which later merged with Benz & Cie. to produce the Mercedes-Benz line of cars.

Military

Jürgen Stroop (September 26, 1895 — March 6, 1952)

Nazi SS officer Jürgen Stroop was sentenced to death for his war crimes in the liquidation of the

Warsaw Ghetto, and was hanged by Polish authorities in 1952.

Notable Casualties of the Battle of the Alamo (varied — March 6, 1836)

Jim Bowie (born c. 1796)
Davy Crockett (born August 17, 1786)
William Travis (born August 1, 1809)

Music

Nelson Eddy (June 29, 1901 — March 6, 1967)

Classically trained baritone Nelson Eddy is best known for his eight operetta films with soprano Jeanette MacDonald, beginning with 1935's *Naughty Marietta*.

John Philip Sousa (November 6, 1854 — March 6, 1932)

Known as the "March King" for his many American military and patriotic marches, John Philip Sousa conducted the U. S. Marine Band and invented the sousaphone.

John Philip Sousa

Constanze Mozart (January 5, 1762 — March 6, 1842)

Constanze Mozart was the wife of composer Wolfgang Amadeus Mozart.

Politics and Law

Anne Braden (July 28, 1924 — March 6, 2006)

Anne Braden grew up in a white middle-class family in Anniston, Alabama, and repudiated her culture's belief in racial segregation to become a significant supporter of the civil rights movement during the 1950s and 1960s. She received the ACLU's Roger Baldwin Medal of Liberty for her work.

Michael Manley (December 10, 1924 — March 6, 1997)

Michael Manley was the fourth prime minister of Jamaica.

Oliver Wendell Holmes, Jr. (March 8, 1841 — March 6, 1935)

Associate Supreme Court Justice Oliver Wendell Holmes, Jr., is one of the most cited American legal scholars of the 20th century.

Oliver Wendell Holmes, Jr.

Anton Cermak (May 9, 1873 — March 6, 1933)

Chicago mayor Anton Cermak created a powerful political organization in the city. He was shot and killed by assassin Giuseppe Zangara while shaking hands with President-elect Franklin D. Roosevelt. Whether Zangara was aiming at FDR or Cermak remains a matter of controversy.

Religion

Martin Niemöller (January 14, 1892 — March 6, 1984)

Anti-Nazi theologian and Lutheran pastor Martin Niemöller is famous for his statement, "First they came..." He survived imprisonment in the Sachsenhausen and Dachau concentration camps and spent his remaining years as a pacifist and anti-war activist.

Science and Mathematics

Hans Bethe (July 2, 1906 — March 6, 2005)

Nobel Prize winning physicist Hans Bethe headed the Theoretical Division at the Los Alamos laboratory during the Manhattan Project, which developed the first atomic bombs, and made major contributions to astrophysics and quantum electrodynamics.

Ferdinand von Lindemann (April 12, 1952 — March 6, 1939)

Mathematician Ferdinand von Lindemann is best known for his 1882 proof that π (pi) is a transcendental number.

Sports

Kirby Puckett (March 14, 1960 — March 6, 2006)

Minnesota Twins center fielder Kirby Puckett was the franchise's all-time leader in career hits, runs, doubles, and total bases. He was elected to the Baseball Hall of Fame in 2001.

"Slapsie Maxie" Rosenbloom (November 1, 1907 — March 6, 1976)

Former light heavyweight champion boxer Max "Slapsie Maxie" Rosenbloom subsequently became an comic actor and opened the first comedy club, Slapsy Maxie's, in San Francisco and Los Angeles.

Words

Ayn Rand (February 2 [O.S. January 20] — March 6, 1982)

Novelist, philosopher and playwright Ayn Rand is known for her novels *Atlas Shrugged* and *The Fountainhead,* and for her philosophy of Objectivism.

Pearl S. Buck (June 26, 1892 — March 6, 1973)

Pearl S. Buck wrote the best-selling novel *The Good Earth*, winning both the Pulitzer Prize and the Nobel Prize for Literature for her chronicles of Chinese peasant life.

Ross Lockridge, Jr. (April 25, 1914 — March 6, 1948)

Novelist Ross Lockridge is famous for his novel *Raintree County,* considered one of the best American works of the 20th century. He committed suicide shortly after the novel's publication.

Louisa May Alcott (November 29, 1832 — March 6, 1888)

Author Louisa May Alcott is best known for her novel *Little Women.*

The month of March, from the illuminated manuscript *Les Très Riches Heures du duc de Berry*

March: The Third Month

In ancient Rome, March was the first month of the year. As the first month of spring, in the Mediterranean climate it marked the beginning of the military campaign season. That's why March (Martius) is named in honor of Mars, the Roman god of war.

Although the first month of the year was moved back to January sometime during the transition of Rome from a kingdom to a republic (historians differ), March was the first month of the year in Russia until the end of the 15th Century, and is the first month of the year in many other cultures and religions.

In the northern hemisphere, March 1 marks the beginning of meteorological spring. In the southern hemisphere, March is the equivalent of September, making southern hemisphere March the beginning of autumn.

March is one of the seven months that have 31 days in it. March starts on the same day of the week as November every year, and except for leap years starts on the same day as February. March starts on the same day of the week as the previous June except for leap years, and in leap years starts on the same day as the previous September and December.

March in Other Cultures

In Finland, March is called *maaliskuu* (earthy month). In Ukraine, it's *березень* (birch tree). Other names for March include *Lentmonat* (Saxon), *Hyld-monath* (Angles), and *sušec* (Slovene).

March Symbols

Birthstones: Aquamarine and bloodstone, both representing courage.

Aquamarine

Birth Flowers Daffodils

Daffodils in Bagatelle Park, Paris, France

March Events

Honorary months: Presidents, Congresses, and nations around the world issue proclamations recognizing particular months to honor certain causes. These events generally fall in March. (All US unless otherwise noted.)

- National Nutrition Month
- American Red Cross Month
- Women's History Month (celebrated in Canada during October)
- Irish-American Heritage Month
- Colorectal Cancer Awareness Month
- Fire Prevention Month (The Philippines)

Women's Suffrage picket line, 1917

"March Madness": (United States) The NCAA Men's Division I Basketball Championship, popularly known as "March Madness" or the "Big Dance," is a single-elimination tournament to establish the champion college basketball team.

Multi-day events: Some March events span multiple days.

- **Nineteen Day Fast:** (Bahá'í Faith) March 2 through March 20

Movable events: Some events change dates from year to year.

- **Mardi Gras:** French for "Fat Tuesday," this celebration takes place the day before Ash Wednesday, the beginning of the Lenten season. The New Orleans Mardi Gras celebration is perhaps the most famous, but Mardi Gras and the Carnival season (between Ephiphany and Ash Wednesday) are celebrated in many areas with large Catholic populations. Mardi Gras can take place anywhere from February 3 to March 9 in regular years, and from February 4 to March 9 in leap years.

Mardi Gras Night Parade, New Orleans, 2012

- **Casimir Pulaski Day:** (Illinois) The first Monday in March is observed as a holiday in Illinois, in memory of the Revolutionary War cavalry officer born in Poland. Dates range from March 1 to March 7.

March Zodiac Signs

From the perspective of someone on Earth, the Sun appears to move through the sky throughout the year, along a path astronomers call the ecliptic plane. The ecliptic plane is divided into twelve constellations, known as the zodiac, based on traditionally observed patterns of stars. On your birthday, you can't see your constellation, because it's part of the daytime sky.

The zodiac was first developed by Babylonian astronomers about 2,500 years ago. Because they were unaware that the Earth wobbles like a spinning top (a motion known as *precession*), they didn't make allowance for the fact that the Sun's path through the zodiac changes over time.

That means there are now two sets of dates for your birth sign. The *tropical dates* are the original Babylonian dates; the *siderial dates* tell you where the Sun actually appears as it moves along its annual path.

Zodiac signs for March 6 are Aquarius (siderial) and Pisces (tropical).

Aquarius

Tropical January 20 to February 19
Siderial February 12 to March 8 (March 9 in leap years)

Aquarius is one of the oldest recognized constellations, originally representing the Babylonian god Ea. In Latin, Aquarius means "water-carrier," represented in its symbol. In Greek mythology, Aquarius is sometimes associated with Deucalion, who survived a world-cleansing flood. In Chinese astronomy, it is known as the Black Tortoise of the North (北方玄武, Běi Fāng Xuán Wǔ).

In astrology, Aquarius is considered to be masculine and extroverted, and despite the name is an air sign. Aquarians are supposed to be philanthropical, inventive, and individualistic.

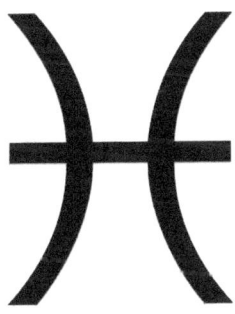

Pisces

Tropical February 20 to March 20
Siderial March 15 to April 14

In the Roman legend of Venus and her son Cupid, they escaped the clutches of Typhon, known as the "father of all monsters," by transforming into fish and tying themselves together with rope. That's why the name Pisces is plural for fish. The constellation appears as a somewhat ragged "V" shape, representing the rope, with the "fish" located at the two rope ends.

In astrology, Pisces is a water sign, compatible with the other water signs Cancer and Scorpio, as well as with the earth signs Taurus, Virgo, and Capricorn. Pisceans are supposed to be imaginative, compassionate, unworldly, secretive, and escapist.

What Day of the Week is March 6?

On what day of the week does March 6 fall?

Unfortunately, this isn't an easy question. Because the calendar year is 365 days long (366 in leap years), it doesn't divide evenly by the seven days of the week.

Also, the Earth goes around the Sun in about 365-1/4 days, so a calendar tends to drift over time. That's why the same date falls on different weekdays in different years.

This is made even more complicated by a change in calendars that took place in 1582. Our modern calendar has its roots in ancient Rome, in a calendar reform conducted by Julius Caesar. Caesar commissioned mathematicians to attack the problem, and came up with the idea of *leap years*, and thus standardized the calendar for centuries to come. This was called the *Julian calendar*.

Over time, however, the small errors in Caesar's calculation compounded. That's why Pope Gregory XIII commissioned the *Gregorian calendar*, used in most of the world today. Some countries converted in 1582, when the calendar was first developed; some converted later; other still haven't changed.

Gregorian and Julian aren't the only types of calendars. The Hebrew year, the Islamic year, and many other calendars are used in different parts of the world and among different people.

You can convert Gregorian dates to other calendars, including the Hebrew calendar, the Islamic calendar, and even the Mayan calendar by visiting the Fourmilab Calendar Converter at http://www.fourmilab.ch/documents/calendar/.

A 50-year brass perpetual calendar.

Copyright, Credit, and Contact

Follow Us

Our blog Dobson's Improbable History features short articles on events and people associated with each day, and updates several times each week. Get the latest on Twitter @SidewiseThinker.

Sources and Art Credits

All art and photographs are either in the public domain or used under a Creative Commons license. Attribution is provided where requested by the copyright owner or when of historical significance, listed below.

- The vector graphic of the face of an Oreo® cookie is by Robb Godshaw, and is used under the terms of the Creative Commons Attribution-Share Alike 3.0 Unported license. The Oreo® design itself is a registered trademark of Nabisco/Kraft Foods.

- The portrait photograph of Muhammad Ali was taken by Ira Rosenberg, a staff photographer of the New York *World-Telegram & Sun* in 1967. It is part of a collection of photographs donated to the Library of Congress. It is in the public domain because the donor dedicated to the public all rights it held.

- The 1976 photograph of Walter Cronkite was taken by a *U. S. News and World Report* photographer. It is part of a collection donated to the Library of Congress, and all rights were dedicated to the public.

- The screenshot of Lou Costello and Hillary Brooke is from the 1949 film *Africa Screams*. It is in the public domain because its copyright was not renewed.

- The 1966 publicity photo of The Supremes is from *The Ed Sullivan Show* and is in the public domain because it was released prior to 1977 without a copyright notice.

- The 2010 photograph of former DC mayor Marion Barry is by D. B. King, and is licensed under the terms of the Creative Commons Attribution 2.0 Generic license.

- The 1781 painting of Henry Laurens is by Lemuel Francis Abbott, and is in the public domain bcause it is an official Congressional portrait prepared by a government employee or contractor.

- The 1969 photograph of cosmonaut Valentina Tereshkova was taken by Alexander Mokletsov. It is from the archives of the Russian International News Agency (RIA Novosti) and is licensed under the terms of the Creative Commons Attribution-Share Alike 3.0 Unported License.

- The official portrait of astronaut Gordon Cooper wearing the Mercury spacesuit was taken in 1962. It is in the public domain because it was created by NASA.

- The 2009 photograph of Shaquille O'Neal was taken by Keith Allison, and is licensed under the Creative Commons Attribution-Share Alike 2.0 Generic License.

- The cover of Will Eisner's *The Spirit* is copyright and trademarked by DC Comics. It is presented here under the fair-use rationale that it (a) illustrates an educational article about the entity it represents, (b) that it is used as the primary means of visual identification of the article topic, (c) that it is a low-resolution image not suitable for the production of counterfeit goods, (d) that it is not used in such a way that a reader would be confused into believing the article is written or authorized by the copyright and trademark owner, and (e) that it is not

59

replaceable with an uncopyrighted or freely copyrighted image of comparable relevance.

- The 1859 engraving of Elizabeth Barrett Browning is by Macaire Havre and T. O. Barlow. It originally appeared in an anthology of her poetry, and is in the public domain because its copyright has expired.

- The detail from Michelangelo's Sistine Chapel ceiling is in the public domain because its copyright has expired.

- The 1942 publicity photograph of Teresa Wright from the film *Mrs. Miniver* is in the public domain because its copyright has expired.

- The image of Georgia O'Keeffe's 1919 painting *Series 1, No. 8* is in the public domain because its copyright is expired.

- The 1932 photograph of the construction of George Washington's likeness at Mount Rushmore is by Rise Studio, Rapid City, South Dakota. It is in the public domain because its copyright was not renewed.

- The 1900 photograph of John Philip Sousa is by Elmer Chickering, and is in the public domain because its copyright is expired.

- The 1924 portrait of Justice Oliver Wendell Holmes was taken by the National Photo Company and is in the collection of the Library of Congress. According to the library, there are no known restrictions on the use of this photograph. It has been cropped for use in this publication.

- The illustration of the month of March is from the French Gothic illuminated manuscript *Les Très Riches Heures du duc de Berry* by the Limbourg Brothers, Jean Colombe, and an intermediate painter whose name is lost to history.

- The photograph of aquamarine has been released into the public domain.

- The photograph of daffodils is by Myrabella, and is licensed under the Creative Commons Attribution-Share Alike 3.0 Unported license.

- The 1917 Women's Suffrage demonstration comes from the Library of Congress, Prints and Photographs Division, LC-USZ62-31799 DLC

- The photograph of the 2012 Mardi Gras Night Parade was taken by Mills Baker, licensed under the Creative Commons Attribution 2.0 Generic License. It has been cropped for use in this publication.

- The 50-year perpetual calendar photograph is in the public domain.